Original title:
Evergreen Elegies

Copyright © 2025 Creative Arts Management OÜ
All rights reserved.

Author: Olivia Sterling
ISBN HARDBACK: 978-1-80567-174-9
ISBN PAPERBACK: 978-1-80567-473-3

Tides of the Transient Seasons

When spring arrives with silly hats,
The trees all laugh and wiggle their spats.
Summer breezes bring a giggle or two,
As squirrels hold court in their sunlit zoo.

Autumn drops leaves with a flamboyant cheer,
Dancing in circles, they're full of good beer.
Winter shakes snow like it's some sort of game,
Trees wear white coats, but they feel no shame.

Secrets of the Somnolent Trunks

Beneath bark armor, naps are profound,
Who knew that trees could snore so loud?
Moss blankets secrets in indolent sleep,
While critters plot jesters' tricks to keep.

A woodpecker giggles in rhythmic pecking,
Calls on the trunks for a joke or two wrecking.
The roots hold gossip, rich tales of delight,
As branches stretch forth in the moonlight's bite.

The Perseverance of the Green

Little sprouts push through the earth's thick crust,
With dreams of sunshine and a bit of rust.
They shake off rain like it's just a fling,
And compete for the spotlight, oh how they sing!

Grass blades huddle for a gossip spree,
Trading tall tales of ants at the spree.
Together they chuckle, nature's comedy,
In the wild theater, they claim their decree.

Melody of the Majestic Pines

Pines sway gently to the breezy tune,
Whispering secrets beneath the bright moon.
They chuckle softly at the naive winds,
As needles dance like a chorus of sins.

Squirrels audition with acrobatic flair,
Each leap and bound shows they haven't a care.
In the majestic shade, laughter's the sound,
Nature's circus where joy knows no bound.

Beneath the Canopy of Solitude

Beneath the trees, a squirrel schemes,
In search of nuts, not ancient dreams.
He stashes food with utmost flair,
While mocking birds just float in air.

The branches sway with laughter bright,
As shadows dance in fading light.
A bear does yoga, quite absurd,
While beetles giggle; oh, how they're heard!

A rabbit reads a book of lore,
While trees gossip; the leaves adore.
The wind whispers jokes from afar,
And nature chuckles under the stars.

Eternal Leaves in Silent Reverie

A leaf fell down; it told a joke,
To passing ants, who simply croak.
They rolled in laughter on the ground,
While clouds above just smiled around.

The daisies nod, they're in on it,
With petals dancing, never quit.
A worm recites his poetry,
While beetles hum in harmony.

The fading light, a soft embrace,
As sunbeams tickle every face.
In leafy tales and laughter grand,
Silly whispers fill the land.

The Resilient Heart of Nature

A cactus stood with prickly pride,
While bunnies hopped, all dignified.
They shared a meal of cactus stew,
And toasted roots with cheers anew.

The sunflowers laughed, a silly sight,
As raindrops danced, oh what a night!
A sloth doing jazz, such a tease,
While ladybugs waltzed with the breeze.

The roots below, they planned a play,
With mushrooms cast for a ballet.
The trees clapped hands, in glee and mirth,
As nature churned its jesting earth.

Melancholy in the Moss

In velvet moss, a snail sings low,
With heartache for a radish, oh!
A frog joins in with croaks of woe,
While butterflies giggle, 'What's the show?'

A hedgehog joins to help out too,
He rolls around, now isn't that true?
While ferns all wave like fans on stage,
Acting out their leafy rage.

The moon sneers down, a cheeky light,
As shadows play their games at night.
Together they weave tales so grand,
Of quirky lives in a mossy land.

Veins of the Gnarled Branches

In the wood, the owls hoot,
Sipping drinks from acorn cups.
Squirrels chatter without a care,
Claiming branches like they own up.

Trees twist like grandmas dance,
With limbs that wiggle and wave.
A squirrel with a dapper hat,
Says, "I'm too cute to misbehave!"

Hushed Tales of the Wildwood

A fox told tales of moonlit jogs,
While snails raced in slow motion.
Bears were belly-laughing loud,
In this absurd woodland notion.

Rabbits wearing tiny shoes,
Came tap dancing on the grass.
They pranced and leaped in rhythm's groove,
Singing 'we're too fast to pass!'

The Forgotten Canopy's Heartbeat

Leaves giggle in breezy chats,
As branches stroke the vibrant sky.
A bird tried to play hide and seek,
But forgot where the tree tops lie.

The moon peeked through treetop cracks,
As fireflies played dazzling pranks.
"Tag, you're it!" the shadows laughed,
While trees just swayed like wobbly tanks.

The Timeless Dance of Leaves

In a whirl of colors bright,
The leaves twirled like dancers bold.
Each step a tumble, a clumsy flight,
That made the morning sun behold.

A gust of wind gave a loud cheer,
As acorns bounced with bouncy glee.
The forest echoed with this song,
"Come join our dance, oh you and me!"

The Last Breath of the Forest

The trees conspired, what a riot,
They whispered secrets, oh so quiet.
The squirrels giggled, oh what fun,
As branches danced beneath the sun.

Leaves shared tales of yore and glee,
Of acorns that wobbled like a bee.
In bark and bough, they made a pact,
To prank the yonder lumberjack.

With every sigh, the forest yawned,
And birds in rapture, sang beyond.
The dew dropped jokes on ferns below,
As critters chuckled in a show.

They staged a play, a leafy farce,
The finale brought a cawing chorus!
For in the end, who would debate,
That nature loves to celebrate?

Murmurs Beneath the Verdant Veil

Beneath the leaves, a gossip flows,
Where petals blush and sunlight glows.
The shadows giggle, tingle-chirps,
While little bugs perform their quirks.

The vines entwined, a dance begun,
They tripped on roots, just for fun.
A wise old tree cracked a sly grin,
As brambles tumbled, hearts akin.

With whispers of mischief, winds confessed,
The mushrooms chuckled, feeling blessed.
For in the shroud of green so tight,
Laughter echoed through the night.

Every rustle, a playful tease,
As creatures shared their tales with ease.
In this embrace, the joy unfurls,
A serenade in leafy whirls.

Elegy of the Enduring Foliage

Oh how the branches sway and creak,
With jokes so old, they seldom speak.
A mossy bard strummed his wet tune,
  Under the gnarled, grinning moon.

The flowers snickered, dancing bright,
  In colors bold, they'd start a fight.
  As petals traded playful blows,
And butterflies donned silly clothes.

"Still here we stand!" the oaks declared,
"Despite the winds and all we've bared!"
  With laughter etched in rings of age,
  They recited tales from every page.

  For nature's jest is never done,
  With every turn, there's more to run.
So join the feast, come take a chance,
  In leafy realms of silly dance.

Petals in the Quiet Breeze

In breezy whispers, petals play,
They flutter softly, drift away.
Each gust a joke, a playful tease,
As nature chuckles with such ease.

The daisies wink, the sunflowers bow,
While nature's friends take quirky vows.
To spin and twirl at every chance,
In fields of laughter, join the dance.

With starlit giggles in the night,
The crickets chirp in pure delight.
As shadows sway and branches sway,
They craft a tale that's here to stay.

So let's embrace this merry tune,
And find our laughter 'neath the moon.
For life's a jest, a grand charade,
With every bloom, a memory made.

Spirits of the Ceaseless Grove

In the grove where squirrels dance,
Fungi sing and take a chance.
Owls wear glasses, tree trunks laugh,
Nature's humor in a photograph.

Ghosts in flannel, don't you see?
Laughing ghosts sip herbal tea.
They tickle leaves with every breeze,
Whisper jokes with subtle ease.

Mice in suits, they run the show,
Chasing shadows, just for a glow.
Acorns roll like bowling balls,
Echoing through nature's halls.

In this forest of pure delight,
Balloons float in the dappled light.
Every branch plays peek-a-boo,
Join the laughter, it's waiting for you!

Reflection in the Shaded Hollow

In a hollow deep and grand,
Frogs in tuxedos start a band.
With lily pad concerts, they engage,
Nature's own comical stage.

Reflection ripples in the pond,
Rabbits hopping, so fond and blonde.
A fish jokes, 'I'm a flying whale!'
While turtles race without a trail.

Squirrels debate on acorn wars,
Their nutty strategies, like old scores.
With each theft, a grinning act,
They play their hands with a sly impact.

Underneath a shady tree,
Join the fun, it's plain to see.
Nature's laughter fills the air,
In this hollow, joy's everywhere!

Shadows of the Stalwart Trees

Beneath the broad and bouncy boughs,
Trees wear hats, and take their bows.
Their shadows dance, a sight to see,
With roots that wiggle, full of glee.

A raccoon plays a clever prank,
In a hat that's quite the crank.
While shadows stretch and twist in jest,
Each leaf whispers, 'Take a rest!'

Woodpeckers drum a lively beat,
While beetles boogie on tiny feet.
The trunks chuckle at this ballet,
Laughter echoes through the day.

Among these shadows, giggles swell,
With every breeze, we cast a spell.
The trees stand tall, yet sway with cheer,
Join the party; you're welcome here!

Sighs of the Timeless Underbrush

In the underbrush, whispers rise,
Where bushes chuckle and pine trees sigh.
Bumblebees wear tiny crowns,
While hedgehogs roll in leafy gowns.

Snails on scooters race with flair,
A slippery slope, but who does care?
In this chaos of nature's play,
Every critter has a role today.

Underneath the bramble thick,
A chicken plays a magic trick.
With feathers bright and laughter loud,
She draws an ever-curious crowd.

As twilight settles, twinkling bright,
The underbrush becomes the night.
Nature's sighs are filled with cheer,
In this timeless space, you'll find good humor here!

Legacy of the Whispering Woods

In the woods where squirrels dance,
Trees gossip, as leaves prance.
A raccoon in a hat so grand,
Sips acorns, like a true connoisseur's brand.

The owl hoots with a wink and stare,
Joking 'bout foxes with secret flair.
Branches tickle each other tight,
While shadows wiggle, what a sight!

Flame and Frost Among the Roots

Sunshine giggles, frost gives chase,
As squirrels play a game of grace.
Nature's flames with icy breath,
Compete, but it's all in jest, no death.

The rabbit wears a scarf of green,
Protesting winter, what a scene!
With every jump, a joke unfolds,
In laughter's warmth, the chill now molds.

Requiem of the Hollowed Bark

A tree stands tall, its bark a clown,
With knotholes laughing all around.
Echoes of giggles float on by,
While birds in suits prepare to fly.

Woodpeckers drum a silly tune,
Raccoons dance under a silver moon.
In this hollowed home of cheer,
Nature's story brings us near.

Sentinels of the Lush Wild

Watch the trees, they're standing tall,
Rooted guardians, they see it all.
Buzzy bees in tiny hats,
Join the party, imagine that!

Whispers echo through leafy halls,
Squirrels juggle, laughter calls.
In this wild, all's fair game,
Every creature, a funny name.

Ink on Celestial Bark

Inky skies above my head,
My thoughts drift like a sled.
Stars giggle at my clumsy pen,
Scribbling once, and then again.

Branches wave, 'What's that noise?'
I swear it's just the trees' joys.
Their whispers tickle every night,
Reminding me to get it right.

Leaves are giggling, what a sound!
Echoes of my words abound.
I wrote a verse about a tree,
And now it's mocking me with glee!

Cosmic canvas, oh what fun,
With every blob, my stress is done.
But watch out for that squirrel brigade,
Trying to edit my grand parade!

Sorrow Beneath the Everbark

Underneath the snickering pines,
Lies a sadness that intertwines.
Yet roots are laughing as they grow,
'We've seen worse, don't be so low!'

A tear drips from a gnarled trunk,
But nearby, there's an old punk.
'You call that sorrow? That's a jest!
Cheer up, my friend, it's a fun quest!'

Crickets chirp their witty rhymes,
At dusk's bizarre, awkward climes.
With every sob, a giggle swells,
Even the great oaks can tell.

Lamenting sighs turn to delight,
As fireflies dance in sheer fright.
Embrace the laughter, let it soar,
For beneath the bark, joy's at the core!

Memories Cradled in the Evergreen

In a hug of branches, memories nest,
Tickling minds when they're at rest.
A squirrel's chase, a raccoon's dance,
Each moment shimmers, given a chance.

Giggles echo through the air,
As stories whisper, everywhere.
'Remember the time we lost our hats?
In the rush of those cheeky bats?'

Leaves flutter like laughter shared,
No burden here, none ever cared.
"Did you hear about the tree that snored?"
Its bark cracked up; the roots adored.

Together they weave, with teasing looks,
Funny tales from nature's books.
In the embrace of green, we find,
Joyful echoes, sweet and kind!

The Guardian's Lament

A guardian stands with a crooked grin,
Swallows deep sorrow, lets the laughs in.
'Am I a tree or a grumpy sage?
With each passing hour, I flip the page!'

Barking up all the wrong trees,
'Do I hold wisdom, or just allergies?'
The woodpeckers laugh at my big dilemma,
They tease, 'Oh, just join our little schema!'

I wear owl glasses, but can't see straight,
In the world of trees, it's never too late.
Lament but chuckle, tiptoe through gales,
'What's worse than silence? Missing the tales!'

With seeds of humor I guard this grove,
Finding joy in whispers, the trees know.
So if you hear a giggle in bark,
Just know I'm listening—my duty, my spark!

Portraits Beneath the Bough

Gather 'round the ancient tree,
Where squirrels hold their jubilee.
A portrait hangs, quite askew,
    Of a raccoon in a tutu.

With branches swaying side to side,
A cozy home for worms to hide.
In the shade, a chipmunk sips,
While gossip flows through leafy quips.

If leaves could laugh, oh what a sound,
As roots conspire beneath the ground.
Nature's jests, a playful show,
Under the bough, the humor flows.

Timeless Mourning in Nature's Choir

The flowers weep, what a surprise,
With petals drooping like sad eyes.
Bees buzz in a somber hum,
Till daisies dance, and drums go thrum!

The wind sings tales of old delight,
Of silly frogs in a moonlit flight.
While weeping willows sag and bend,
Their tears might just be a prank, my friend!

Birds chirp tunes of woe and cheer,
As butterflies flit near and near.
In nature's choir, the laughter swells,
Between sorrowful tales, joy always dwells.

Hymn of the Immortal Saplings

Saplings stand, tall and spry,
Making poses to the sky.
A frog leaps high, a crowd goes wild,
While sunbeams shine on nature's child.

Roots are tangled in a dance,
As young buds take a daring chance.
Their shadows mock, a silly sight,
While ants march on with pure delight.

Old trees whisper, 'What's the fuss?'
'You saplings think you're quite the plus!'
But laughter rings through air so sweet,
In nature's hymn, the rhymes repeat.

Fanfare of Forever Green

The trumpet of the pine trees calls,
As mossy carpets soften falls.
With every gust, the branches sway,
A fanfare brightens the gray day.

The ferns do a jig, the lichen claps,
As nature giggles, no need for maps.
In the shade, the mushrooms jest,
While butterflies put on their best.

A symphony of laughs abounds,
In every rustle, nature's sounds.
Through all the green, the humor gleans,
In this forever flourishing scene.

Chronicles of the Wind-Kissed Willows

In springtime's jest, the willows sway,
With whispers soft, they dance and play.
A squirrel in socks, he hops with glee,
While bees wear shades, sipping herbal tea.

Beneath the boughs, the critters gather,
Telling tall tales that end in laughter.
A raccoon with dreams of being a star,
Practices lines from a film bizarre.

The breezy jokes, the way it tickles,
Even the grass cracks up with giggles.
A spider spins webs of laughter's thread,
In this leafy realm where humor is spread.

Yet come the fall, while leaves are shy,
The willows chuckle, waving goodbye.

The Spirit of the Evergreen Oasis

In a lush retreat where giggles sprout,
The pines play puns that twist about.
A cactus in shades gives a wink,
'Don't hug too tight, or I'll make you think!'

The ferns stomp feet like tap dance pros,
While creeks gurgle jokes that nobody knows.
A moose with style, wearing a tie,
Struts through the oasis, oh my, oh my!

The air is thick with chortling sighs,
As laughter bubbles under sunny skies.
In this haven bright, cheer is the rule,
Even the rocks are breaking school!

But dusk will fall, and tales will cease,
Yet laughter echoes like a sweet release.

Verses Among the Cedar Stands

In a cedar grove where giggles bloom,
A woodpecker taps out a funky tune.
Squirrels debate what is best to eat,
Pinecones or nuts, oh what a feat!

The sun peeks through with its playful grin,
While the raccoons plan their next silly win.
A hedgehog rolls in a barrel of leaves,
Claiming, 'I'm fashion, it's autumn that cleaves!'

Whispers of secrets in a rustling breeze,
As the trees shake branches, entwined with tease.
A fox tells riddles that take some time,
While mushrooms sprout, enhancing the rhyme.

Yet as night falls, the laughter will fade,
In the cedar stands, where memories are made.

Notes from the Ageless Arbor

The ancient oak, with wisdom or two,
Cracks a dad joke, a favorite to rue.
'Knock knock,' it starts, the birds all chirp,
'Who's there?' oh dear, it makes my head slurp!

A family of deer giggle in line,
Pondering if they're lost, oh so fine.
While butterflies tease the flowers they pass,
'Catch me if you can,' they boldly amass.

The wind carries tales, both silly and bright,
While shadows dance under the moonlight.
In the heart of the woods, joy's never sparse,
As the ageless arbor becomes a lively farce.

But time ticks on, and the merriment must fade,
Leaving behind the humor they made.

Vows of the Vast Wilderness

In the woods where the squirrels play,
Bears dance silly, come what may.
Trees chuckle while the leaves all cheer,
Nature's comedy, oh so clear.

Raccoons in masks, a heist in mind,
Stealing snacks of every kind.
Owls roll their eyes, and hoot with glee,
An acorn fest? Count me in, you see!

Mushrooms giggle beneath the sun,
Saying, "Life's too short, let's have some fun!"
Dancing in the breeze, the grass wears crowns,
Nature's humor: it tickles, it frowns.

Each twig a joker, each stone a sage,
Crafting jokes on nature's stage.
In this vast wild, laughter's the tune,
Even the night fox grins at the moon.

Rhapsody of the Timeless Glade

In a glade where shadows prance,
Chirping crickets start to dance.
A turtle walks with swagger slight,
Saying, "I'm fast—just not tonight!"

Breezes breeze with puns galore,
Flowers gossip, sharing lore.
A dandelion's wish, "What a laugh!"
As bees buzz by, they stop for a chat.

The sunset blushes, paints the sky,
While frogs croak jokes, oh my, oh my!
A rabbit winks, with a cheeky grin,
"When life is tough, just hop and spin!"

Moss drops quips, "I'm soft, I'm wise,
Stick with me, let's share some fries."
In this rhapsody, all's delight,
Where whispers humor through the night.

Whispers of Timeless Woods

In the woods where shadows play,
Trees gossip the livelong day.
A fox wearing glasses, reading a map,
Says, "I'm not lost, I just adapt!"

Mice gather round for a small soirée,
With crumbs and giggles in their array.
Woodpeckers joke with a tap and a knock,
"Let's share our stories, let's take stock!"

A brook bubbling with laughter clear,
Says, "I flow better when friends are near!"
Sunlight winks, and shadows tease,
Nature's jesters, they aim to please.

In this whispering woodland joke,
Each leaf a giggle, each branch bespoke.
Through timeless realms where laughter's spun,
The heart of nature beats with fun.

Lament of the Silent Pines

The pines stand tall, a somber sight,
Whispering tales to the moonlit night.
Yet in their whispers, a chuckle forms,
"Life's just a joke with various norms!"

Beneath their boughs, a party planned,
With nimble deer and a fun parade.
A skunk in a tie, with a flower flair,
Says, "Don't worry, I'll freshen the air!"

Each twig bent down to tickle the ground,
While porcupines dance without a sound.
Lamenting softly, but laughter drips,
For even silence enjoys some quips.

The forest sighs, but it's not all doom,
Nature's humor reveals its bloom.
In the pines, where secrets dwell,
Laughter layers each leafy shell.

Serenade of the Immortal Boughs

In the woods where squirrels jest,
The branches dance, a leafy fest.
Old oaks chuckle, moss in tow,
They tell tales of long-lost snow.

The pines wear hats made of the sky,
While rabbits hop with a wink and sigh.
A squirrel's prank – he swings and spins,
Bouncing off the bark, he grins.

The trees gossip, roots intertwined,
Whispering secrets, one of a kind.
With every breeze, they start to sway,
And pinecones fall like confetti play.

The sun peeks through, a chuckling light,
As trees hold court from dawn till night.
A symphony of giggles and glee,
In this woodland, wild and free.

Echoes in the Eternal Canopy

Under leaves that paint the sky,
A woodpecker's tap is the laugh on high.
Branches nod in rhythmic cheer,
As whispers of wind dance near.

Laughter bubbles from bubbling brooks,
While ancient trees share funky looks.
A beetle struts in a tiny parade,
With all of nature in grand charade.

Sunbeams play tag with shadows wide,
As squirrels plot their next wild ride.
The bamboo sways, in jest and tease,
Making friends with the teasing breeze.

Echoes of chuckles, a playful song,
In this enclave, where we belong.
The canopy hums, the branches lean,
In a world of green, so whimsical and keen.

Ode to the Timeless Thicket

In thickets where the snails take their time,
The flowers burst out, a colorful rhyme.
A hedgehog rolls, a curious sight,
With laughter spun from morning's light.

A dandelion offers a wish to the breeze,
While bumblebees dance, with such elegance and ease.
Every rustle brings a chuckle to the air,
As nature blooms in whimsical flair.

Moss-covered rocks hold secret tales,
Of wobbly creatures and vegetable trails.
With every rustling, joy ignites,
In this thicket, where mirth delights.

The rabbits play hopscotch, the frogs leap high,
While the sun spills laughter across the sky.
In every nook, joy takes its stand,
In this timeless wonderland.

Memories of the Weathered Leaf

A leaf drops down, with a laugh of grace,
Gliding slowly, it knows its place.
It swirls and twirls, what a sight to see,
Sharing secrets with the dancing bee.

The old tree chuckles, shedding its wear,
As autumn's palette combs through the air.
"Look at me!" says a branch, so shifty,
"I'm sprucing up and feeling nifty!"

The gusts of wind play tag with the bark,
As the sun sets low, igniting a spark.
Memories linger, a flutter of cheer,
As the reminisce drifts far and near.

In this forest, laughter weaves and separates,
From weathered leaves to jubilant states.
Each rustle recounts a jubilant day,
In a world where fun will always stay.

The Call of the Wildwood Spirit

In a forest where raccoons roam,
A squirrel found a shiny chrome.
He danced like a king, it's a sight to behold,
With a nutty crown, oh so bold.

The oaks laughed at his foolish flair,
While birds chirped gossip up in the air.
'What's next?' hooted an owl with glee,
'A disco ball for us to see?'

Beneath the moon, the shadows play,
The critters celebrate a wild ballet.
With mischief and laughter echoing wide,
The wildwood spirit is their guide.

So if you wander where trees entwine,
Keep an ear out for the giggles divine.
For nature's jesters are always quite spry,
In the magical woods where the laughter won't die.

The Winds Whisper Through the Pines

The winds tangle up the branches high,
Making the pine trees wave goodbye.
'Hey there!' they holler, 'Catch a breeze!'
The whole forest starts to tease.

A chipmunk wearing a tiny hat,
Swings from a branch like a furry acrobat.
With each gust, he performs a flip,
While the dandelions blow a jaunty trip.

The pines sigh sweetly, their secrets shared,
They know where the wild things are ensnared.
With laughter twinkling in every gust,
It's a woodland party, in nature we trust!

So if you find yourself lost in a breeze,
Remember the trees dancing with ease.
Join in the fun, be fleeting and free,
Where whispers of joy are the key.

Half-Remembered Chronicles of the Woodlands

Once upon a time, the trees would talk,
About a frog who could surf and walk.
He rode the streams like a pro on a board,
Saying, 'Nature's a party, come join the hoard!'

The owls held meetings, discussing the best,
Of pinecone piñatas and beetle quests.
The forest was lively with tales that inspired,
Of critters and capers that never retired.

Each breeze would carry a whimsical tale,
Of dancing mushrooms and a snail with a sail.
The stories are jumbled, but laughter is here,
Echoing through branches, bringing us cheer.

So listen closely to whispers at night,
Where humor and nature unite in delight.
For in this realm of oddities fine,
We share in the joy of an obscure design.

Colors of Nature's Continuous Cycle

The daisies wore yellow for a garden dance,
While the violets giggled, caught in a trance.
'Look at us!' they chimed with glee,
'Nature's palette is wild and free!'

A butterfly flitted, all dressed in style,
Showing off colors that sparkled a mile.
The trees rolled their eyes, as leaves turned red,
'It's just a phase; soon they'll be dead!'

But every season, there's a joke or two,
As we watch the green fade to gray and blue.
With a wink and a nod, the blooms fade away,
And start again fresh in the merry month of May.

So cheer for the hues, and laugh at the change,
For nature's comedy is wildly strange.
In every shade and each twist of the vine,
The colors of life brightly intertwine.

The Last Leaf's Farewell

Once I was green and spry,
Now I dangle, oh so shy.
The wind whispers with a grin,
"Time to dance before the spin!"

I wish I had a sturdy grip,
But alas, I'm ready to slip.
My fellow leaves shout, "Don't be meek!"
Yet here I am, a fading cheek.

I'd fall in style, with flair and twist,
A grand finale, can't resist!
A leaf that's lived, now takes a bow,
"Watch out, world! Here comes the how!"

So off I go, a brave retreat,
With every gust, a new heartbeat.
The ground below will be my stage,
A leaf's last laugh as I disengage.

In the Heart of the Immutable Forest

In the woods where shadows play,
Trees gossip in a funny way.
They chuckle at the squirrels' stunts,
And tease the birds out on their hunts.

Amidst the trunks, a party brews,
With acorns, nuts, and funky shoes.
The raccoons joke, "Who wears a tie?"
While owls give side-eyes, oh my, oh my!

A chubby beetle writes a book,
Its title: 'How to Be a Nook'.
The porcupines roll in delight,
As fireflies twinkle through the night.

Here laughter rings in every nook,
Even hedgehogs have their own look.
In this forest, life's a tease,
Come join the fun, if you please!

Where Time Stands Still

In this realm where clocks forget,
We dance and sing, no chance of fret.
The grass giggles, "Stay awhile!"
While clouds drift by with a lazy smile.

A turtle claims it's first in line,
While squirrels pen a script divine.
"Who needs a rush?" they chant with glee,
As time stands still beneath the tree.

The mushrooms laugh at fungi jokes,
Their spores erupt in witty pokes.
With every hour, they grow and bloom,
In this stillness, joy finds room.

So take a breath and join the slot,
In slow-motion, give it a shot.
In a world where tick-tocks chill,
Live large in joy, with time to fill.

The Resilience of Saplings

Small but mighty, we do appear,
With wobbly roots but a hearty cheer.
"Look at us," we laugh and sing,
Ready to embrace the joys of spring!

"Who needs storms?" we chirp and squeal,
With every gust, we start to feel.
Though winds may bend, they can't break us,
As we giggle in the green bus.

While towering giants grumble and moan,
We prancing sprouts steal the show alone.
With every leaf, we're on a quest,
To prove that tiny can be the best.

So here we stand, boldly arrayed,
In dances crisp, our roots displayed.
With chuckles deep, we take our stand,
The forest floor beneath our band.

Secrets of the Ageless Glade

In the glade where secrets dwell,
Whispers make the pine trees yell.
The squirrels laugh at cheesy jokes,
As mushrooms dance with their blushing cloaks.

In shadows where the shadows hide,
Old oaks gossip with great pride.
They chuckle 'bout the morning dew,
While rabbits scoot with madcap view.

A fox struts past with a silly grin,
Bragging 'bout the mess he's in.
He tripped on roots and lost his shoe,
But hey, who'd notice? Just ask the crew!

The breeze carries laughter far and wide,
As nature's jesters take their ride.
In this crack-up of leafy cheers,
They share their punchlines through the years.

The Solitary Cedar's Song

A cedar stands, all alone and proud,
Singing songs that aren't too loud.
He croons of acorns and nuts galore,
Of silly tales, who could ask for more?

The owls roll their eyes at his old-time lyrics,
While chipmunks giggle, displaying their quirks.
"Hey Cedar, that tune is such a bore,"
But he just laughs, "I got a million more!"

He sways and bends with rhythm so grand,
Dreaming of dance-offs in this woodland band.
But all alone, he spins in place,
A solo show with a comical grace.

Yet when the moonlight fills the night:
He tells secrets that laugh in fright.
Around this cedar, merry jests fly,
Stirring the leaves with a playful sigh.

In the Realm of Verdant Spirits

In the realm where green things play,
Mossy sprites cause quite a fray.
They tickle stumps and tease the ferns,
As laughter in the woodland turns.

A spirit trips and falls with glee,
Right into a laughing spree.
The vines all twist in twinkling light,
While fireflies blink, "Oh what a sight!"

Here even trees roll up their bark,
As critters snap selfie sparks.
The stream gurgles, "Let's make a scene!"
Announcing the fun, each swell and sheen.

In whispers soft, the breezes share,
Of days gone by with silly flair.
With every rustle, chuckles bolt,
In the realm where joy's the main revolt.

Echoes of the Forest's Heartbeat

In the forest, where echoes dwell,
Trees chuckle softly, a verdant swell.
A parrot squawks out jokes anew,
While rabbits roll, all in a stew.

Mushrooms peek from their leafy beds,
Gossiping 'bout what tickles their heads.
"Did you hear what that fox once wore?
A jacket made from a raccoon's door!"

The brooks bubble with mock surprise,
As crickets croon with sparkling eyes.
"Have you seen the hare try to jump?
He landed straight on a ladybug's lump!"

Echoes bounce with laughter bold,
In every tale that nature's told.
In this heart where mirth takes flight,
The forest beams with pure delight.

Guardian of the Glimmering Glade

In the woods, a gnome stands tall,
Hiding treats behind a tree's wall.
Squirrels giggle, mischief they wield,
While he guards his enchanted field.

With mushrooms dancing in delight,
He twirls and spins, a curious sight.
The fairies laugh, they take a bow,
For who knew gnomes could dance like how?

Sipping dew from a tiny cup,
He cheers the leaves, "Come on, get up!"
The sunlight breaks, he starts to sing,
As nature laughs at his silly fling.

In golden light, the glades do cheer,
With antics wild, they close the year.
As twilight whispers, they thank their friend,
In this glimmering space that will never end.

The Thinker Amidst the Firs

Beneath the pines, a wise owl blinks,
Contemplating life as it quietly thinks.
He scribbles notes on a bark so clean,
While critters gather, curious, keen.

"Should I hoot? Or join the crowd?"
Marginalized in thoughts so loud.
The chipmunks chuckle, with why and how,
"Just say something! You're wise, but wow!"

With branches scratching his feathery head,
He ponders on dreams while softly spread.
His solution? A dance in the air,
Flapping his wings without a care.

At dusk, he flies, light as a plume,
Becoming a riddle that soon finds bloom.
The wisdom of owls may seem quite grand,
But all they need is a soft, warm band.

The Color of Endless Seasons

Leaves turn gold and then to brown,
While squirrels, in scarves, scurry around.
Colors collide in a crazy spree,
With trees wearing shades of jubilee.

The maples chuckle, the oaks play tag,
While pinecones giggle, ready to brag.
Winter arrives with a chilly grin,
Snowball fights where laughter begins.

As springtime blossoms in a rush,
The flowers gossip in no such hush.
Colors of rainbows spread with glee,
Nature's palette, a sight to see.

Seasons dance in whimsical pride,
Each twist and turn, by joy, they abide.
Endless laughter in colors bright,
Nature's jesters in sweet daylight.

Guardian of the Verdant Horizon

On the horizon, a tree stands bold,
Guarding secrets, both new and old.
With roots entwined in devlish fun,
It whispers jokes to the warming sun.

A hedgehog laughs, napkin in hand,
As grasshoppers play in a jubilant band.
The breeze carries tales of absurd deeds,
While the flower crowns collect nature's seeds.

Bees share puns that make daisies sway,
As butterflies flutter in bright array.
The twilight winks, the moon sneezes bright,
"Bless you!" said the stars, in the cool night light.

In this realm with a vibrant hue,
Nature's guardians are silly too.
Together they dance, laughing till dawn,
Under the sky where dreams are drawn.

Fragments of Nature's Monologue

Leaves gossip under the sun's bright glow,
Squirrels debate, who steals the show.
The bark gets tickled by a playful breeze,
While ants march forth with utmost ease.

Mushrooms are sneaky, just peek and you'll see,
They plot a grand party; who'll bring the brie?
The grass chuckles softly, trying to act coy,
As flowers take selfies, oh, what a ploy!

Crickets compose with a scratchy old tune,
While owls critique from under the moon.
The wise, wise trees nod, their branches so long,
Who knew nature's whispers could yield such a song?

So next time you wander through the leafy expanse,
Remember the laughter, the jokes, and the dance.
The world's full of humor in every green space,
Nature's a jester, oh, what a place!

Gleam of the Dusk-Kissed Pines

Dusk wraps the pines in a warm, cozy hug,
While critters conspire from the heart of the mug.
A bear in a tutu waltzes with grace,
And owls chant sonnets, each verse a new case.

The moon sneezes softly, a misty surprise,
As shadows and giggles say secret goodbyes.
One fox wears a hat, how dapper he looks,
While skunks hold a meeting with old dusty books.

The stars sprinkle stories, a twinkling delight,
While crickets in tuxedos prepare for the night.
Rabbits throw carrots like javelins so sleek,
While the forest erupts in a whimsical peak.

In this dusk-kissed kingdom where laughter ignites,
Nature's bright humor shines through the long nights.
So listen intently, let joy be your guide,
For every tree chuckles; you just have to confide.

Immortal Stories in the Thicket

In the thicket of tales where the wild things roam,
Each shrub spins a yarn from its leafy old home.
A raccoon narrates with a flagon of jam,
While hedgehogs applaud, their quills raised in glam.

The thorns weave a drama, oh, what a scene,
Where daisies play lead, and the thistles intervene.
The bramble takes stage; it's a prickly affair,
As the butterflies flutter without a single care.

Dandelions blow, spreading secrets like seeds,
While the vibrant tulips share gossip with reeds.
In a world full of chatter, each plant has a voice,
And everyone giggles – no need to rejoice!

So next time you find yourself lost in a bush,
Remember the stories, the laughter that swush.
Immerse in the fun where nature acts bold,
In forests of whimsy, the tales are retold.

The Embrace of the Verdant Overgrowth

In the lush, leafy embrace where wild things convene,
The vines are all tangled, like threads of a scene.
A frog in a crown holds court with a grin,
While daisies in chaos hold hands in a spin.

The moss throws a party, a pillow-like spread,
For beetles in bowties, all stunningly bred.
While ladybugs play tag in a game of delight,
The thicket erupts into giggles that night.

Lily pads gossip, they're in on a scheme,
While mushrooms with shades plot a raucous dream.
The ferns form a chorus, oh, what a surprise,
With melodies soaring beneath the full skies.

So dance in the jungle where laughter entwines,
Amidst zany critters and high-spirit signs.
For nature's a circus, where joy is the thread,
In the embrace of growth, let the hilarity spread!

Yearning of the Wandering Souls

Lost in the woods, they roam in delight,
Searching for snacks, 'til the end of the night.
With dreams full of cheese, and paths that are sly,
These hungry souls dance, and oh, how they try!

Spooky old whispers, they tickle their ears,
"Where's that ghost pizza?" asks one with no fears.
They brush past the branches, so lively, so free,
But lunch breaks are rare, oh how could this be?

A gathering clash 'neath the twinkling stars,
With cookies and brownies, the best of fine bars!
The wandering souls, with their sweet tooth in tow,
Prepare for a feast, oh the laughter will flow!

Yet daylight approaches, their fun's nearly done,
A sad little wave—oh! They had so much fun!
Ghostly goodbyes as they waltz through the trees,
We'll see them next time for some snacks and some cheese!

Ghosts Among the Evergreens

In the forest depths, where the shadows play,
Ghosts try to scare folks, yet more often they sway.
"Boo!" cries a phantom, with a grin on his face,
But a squirrel scoffs back, not giving him space!

With chains made of cobwebs, they rattle and roll,
While deer pass on by, they don't give a goal.
"Is that all you've got?" says a ghost with a wink,
As sprites start a dance, and the owls stop to blink.

An old ghostly shindig, they burst into song,
With didgeridoos, and they dance all night long.
The trees, they are swaying, keeping perfect time,
As crickets play rhythms, in spontaneous rhyme!

But morning light giggles, and shadows take flight,
The ghosts wave goodbye, till the cloak of the night.
With a wink and a chuckle, they promise, "We'll meet!"
In the land of the trees, for a brand-new retreat!

Echoes of the Forest's Heart

In the thicket of laughter, where tall tales abound,
Echoes of mischief in whispers resound.
The trees have a giggle, the leaves share a jest,
With critters conspiring to give us a test!

"Knock, knock!" says Acorn, with a mischievous glow,
"Who's there?" asks a rabbit—oh, little does he know!
It's Chipmunk, old prankster, with a face made of cheese,

He leaps out and dances, "Surprise, if you please!"

The breeze carries secrets, of jests yet untold,
Each rustling branch teases as the stories unfold.
Hoots and chortles echo beneath the sky wide,
Nature's own chorus, with the critters as guide.

But soon the day fades, with the sun's lazy sweep,
Nature settles down—the forest drifts to sleep.
Yet in dreams, they'll gather, around the old bark,
To conjure more giggles, until it gets dark.

The Language of the Leaf

Whispers of leaves, a chatter divine,
Converse with the breezes, in a language of wine.
"Do you hear that rustle?" a leaf claims with pride,
It's just the wind laughing—what a funny ride!

With twirls and with flutters, they spin round the trees,
Dancing like party-goers, hoping for cheese.
One leaf slips and tumbles, a giggle it shares,
Soon he's spinning solo—no worries or cares!

The moss cushions laughter, with soft snickers and glee,
As roots join the party, tapping silently.
The mushrooms stand firm like an audience grand,
Cheering for fun, waving flowers in hand!

But as daylight retreats with its warm amber glow,
The leaves tuck in tight, and the giggles grow slow.
A promise they make, to meet up next spring,
For a leafy revival—what joy it will bring!

Twilight's Caress on the Fir

In twilight's grip, the firs do dance,
They giggle leaves, take every chance.
Squirrels debate who's the best tree,
While raccoons plot mischief, oh so free.

The moon winks down with a silvery grin,
While owls hoot jokes, where should I begin?
The pines breathe in, they're full of sass,
Sharing secrets with every passerby that does trespass.

A rabbit hops in, wearing a hat,
While bees hold a party—imagine that!
The firs shake their boughs, good spirits abound,
Twilight's a prankster, it spreads joy around.

So here's to the moments we laugh, oh what bliss,
Nature's chuckles are hard to dismiss.
In the embrace of those fragrant trees,
Life's funny little quirks bring hearts to tease.

The Memory of Lost Seasons

Once the leaves fell, we laughed all day,
A pile of colors to jump and play.
Each crunch beneath, a symphony sweet,
While squirrels criticized our clumsy feet.

Winter rolled in, and we lost our way,
Snowmen told jokes, in a frosty ballet.
Return of the sun made the daisies fight,
Who'd wear the crown of the brightest light?

We painted the flowers with bubbles and cheer,
Trying to catch winter, but spring was near.
The seasons just chuckled, a droll parade,
For laughter in nature will never fade.

So heed this memory, hold it tight,
Even in gloom, there's always delight.
In the rhythm of nature, we find our cue,
To laugh in the shadows—start anew.

Requiem for the Shaded Grove

In a grove of shadows where jokes intertwine,
Trees share their stories with whimsy divine.
The ghosts of humor float in the air,
Tickling the trunks with a mischievous flair.

A crow caws loudly, "Let's start the fun!"
While a sly young fox declares, "I've just won!"
The moss giggles softly, a whispering tone,
As the trees look on with a chuckle and groan.

Fallen branches, the stage for a play,
Where nature's comedians have their say.
The leaves rustle gently, they know the score,
Humor's an echo, forever in war.

So raise a toast to the grove's happy stand,
Where laughter and shade go hand in hand.
In the heart of the trees, hilarity thrives,
A requiem to joy, where the spirit survives.

Chronicles of the Unfading

In a land where colors refuse to fade,
The flowers conspire in a sunshine parade.
They trade silly puns as the bees buzz along,
While butterflies join in, singing their song.

The trees wear their wrinkles like badges of pride,
Sharing tales of the past, with laughter as guide.
A grumpy old oak claims he's done with the youth,
But he giggles at saplings, can't handle the truth.

Perpetual pranks in this vibrant domain,
Where each twist of fate brings laughter and gain.
The stones roll their eyes at the foolhardy blooms,
For elegance often just adds to the fumes.

So gather around for a tale full of glee,
Of nature's quirks in her jolly decree.
In the chronicles spun 'neath the sun's warm embrace,
Life unfades into humor, a delightful grace.

Reverie of the Ancient Grove

In the heart of the woods, trees weave a tale,
Squirrels in suits tell jokes without fail.
The pinecones laugh as they drop from above,
Nature's own stand-up, a show filled with love.

Mossy old logs hold the secrets of life,
Woodpeckers drum out a rhythm of strife.
"Knock, knock!" they hear, and the trees all chime,
A punchline from nature, oh isn't it prime?

Branches sway gently, like dancers on stage,
Sprightly leaves tease the wind, breaking the cage.
The boughs are in stitches, falling apart,
While the trunks roll their eyes at the jokes from the heart.

Fungi in quirky hats join the fun,
Telling tall tales as the day is begun.
With laughter erupting from every green sprout,
The grove's got a vibe that you can't live without!

Songs of the Unyielding Branches

Beneath the bright sun, the branches conspire,
"Why did the squirrel start a choir?"
"Were they trying to impress the trees?"
With a chorus of chuckles, they sway in the breeze.

The owls wear spectacles, wisdom in sight,
"Any puns about trees? Let's keep it light!"
With leaves whispering secrets and giggles galore,
These ancient seeds know how to explore.

The vines tell stories of thrills and chills,
Entwined in humor, they dance through the hills.
Bamboo takes a bow, says, "I dare you to bend!"
While the willows just giggle, 'cause they're hard to offend.

Laughter resonates through the thicket so thick,
Each branch cracking jokes, oh what a trick!
With the canopy echoing joy all around,
It's a comedy show where no punchline's drowned!

Eulogy for the Forgotten Glade

In a glade that once sang with laughter and cheer,
Now the crickets lament with a froggy veneer.
"Remember the picnics? The fun we all had?"
Now the echoes just bring a touch of the sad.

But wait! Here comes a raccoon on a spree,
With a top hat and monocle, oh can't you see?
"Fear not, dear friends, for I bring a surprise,
A dance-off from shadows, for laughter, we'll rise!"

The flowers are blushing, their petals all bright,
As the raccoon jigs, causing quite the delight.
"In memory of joy, let's throw a grand bash,
With rhymes and with riddles, we'll make fortunes splash!"

So raise up a toast to the glade of yore,
Where the funny times linger, at nature's core.
In every rustling leaf, there's a joke worth the run,
For in the heart of the forest, the laughter weighs a ton!

A Ballad of Resilient Roots

Deep in the soil where the roots intertwine,
A family of plants says, "Oh, isn't life fine?"
"We've weathered the storms, we've danced through the rain,
Why fuss about troubles? Let's jest 'bout the pain!"

The carrots poke fun at the turnip's long nose,
While radishes giggle as the wild garlic grows.
"Do you think we'll be harvested? Oh, dear, what a fright!"
"Not if we hide under the leafy green light!"

With saplings in tow, they're making a scene,
Swinging their stems, all dressed in fresh green.
"We're growing together, just a bunch of old pals,
With roots in the ground, we'll withstand the finals!"

So let's plant some laughter in this garden wide,
Where buds burst with humor and all can abide.
With every new bloom, let the humor take flight,
For in giggles and grins, we'll all be alright!

Silhouettes at Dusk's Embrace

In the twilight's gentle hold,
Trees dance with tales untold.
Squirrels wear tiny shoes,
While crickets hum the blues.

A raccoon dons a tie,
With a top hat, oh my!
He waltzes with a hare,
Through the concert of fresh air.

Bats swoop in for a snack,
Teasing moths in a pack.
The moon laughs with delight,
As shadows take their flight.

Laughter echoes in the breeze,
Rustling leaves like tickling tease.
Nature's jesters come alive,
In dusk's embrace, we thrive.

Shadows of the Old Oak

Under the old oak's watchful gaze,
Laughter echoes through the days.
Pigeons strut in grand parade,
Wearing hats that a child made.

A snail plays the saxophone,
While bugs tap dance on their own.
The gopher steals a bite,
Of acorns, what a sight!

In the rustling leaves, a story,
Of squirrels in their glory.
And frogs sing off-key tunes,
As fireflies join in swoons.

Time winks, tick-tocking slow,
In this whimsical tableau.
The oak can't keep a straight face,
As joy weaves through this space.

Serenade of the Ancient Woods

In ancient woods where whispers weave,
Fairies plot, and mischief cleave.
Trees sport moustaches galore,
While raccoons play on the forest floor.

The owls hoot in uproarious cheer,
Calling all creatures far and near.
A hedgehog sings, off rhythm yet,
To a tune none can forget.

Shadows stretch with playful glee,
Tickling flowers—oh, can't you see?
A worm spins tales of grand design,
In this concert, all align.

In the harmony of night and day,
Nature's jesters come out to play.
Each leaf a note, each root a beat,
In the woods, where laughter meets.

An Ode to Perpetual Bloom

A garden giggles at the dawn,
With flowers wearing crowns of brawn.
Bees in tuxedos buzz about,
Spoiling every sneaky doubt.

Tulips trade their secrets bold,
While daisies share tales of old.
A sunflower spins around with flair,
Pretending it's a great rock star's hair.

The wind hums in rhythmic play,
As butterflies flutter without delay.
Petunias dance on the breeze with glee,
A floral ball, where all are free.

In this vivid, splendid room,
Every stem blooms in sweet perfume.
The garden laughs in splendid light,
In perpetual joy, day and night.

Poetries of the Rooted Realm

In the soil, worms dance, wearing hats,
Singing to trees while picking up chats.
Rabbits in bow ties hopping around,
Trying to serenade the deer with a sound.

Leaves gossip louder than the stream,
Running a rumor, you'd think it's a dream.
Squirrels in spectacles counting their nuts,
Claiming acorns are gold; isn't that nuts?

Barky old trees telling tales of the past,
With bark worse than bite, but never a blast.
Lizards in ties try to look quite prime,
Debating who's faster, the sun or the time.

So dance with the roots, have a good laugh,
Life in the woods is a comical path.
Embrace every joke that the branches may send,
In this rooted realm, there's joy without end.

The Spirit of Nature's Continuity

A turtle in shades is taking a stroll,
Humming a tune with a popcorn bowl.
The clouds overhead are cotton candy,
In this fruity world, everything's dandy.

Frogs in the pond are quite the comedians,
Ribbiting jokes like they're on their meridians.
Butterflies gossip through parties at night,
With disco lights glowing, oh what a sight!

The sunflowers sway, thinking they're smart,
Trying to craft beats straight from the heart.
While bumblebees buzz in infectious delight,
At the flower-karaoke, they sing through the night.

So join in the laughter, let moments unfold,
In harmony's bliss, let the stories be told.
With nature's own spirit, we dance and we sing,
In the laughter of leaves, oh what joy it can bring!

Chronicle of the Boundless Grove

In the grove where the owls wear their capes,
They host a council of giggly bad shapes.
Tree trunks stand tall in their tight little rings,
Listening close for the mischief that sings.

Bunnies in slippers design all their clothes,
Debating on colors for their new toes.
Woodpeckers tapping out a catchy refrain,
While ants keep on marching, ignoring the rain.

The blueberries gossip, their squishy delight,
Sharing the juiciest tales every night.
With a wink and a nod, they plot and they scheme,
In this boundless grove, all's ripe for a dream.

So prance with the critters, clap hands with the breeze,
In the rhythmic embrace of the tall rustling trees.
For in chronicling laughter, the stories unwind,
Within the grove's laughter, there's peace intertwined.

Breath of the Ageless Forest

At dawn, the forest yawns and shakes off the dew,
As raccoons in pajamas celebrate too.
With pinecones for hats, they attend their grand ball,
Whispering secrets from low branches to tall.

Mushrooms giggle as the wind makes a whoosh,
Playing hide and seek with the blossoming bush.
Foxes in frocks discuss matters of old,
While acorns play poker, feeling quite bold.

The brook wears a grin as it flows with finesse,
Tickling the pebbles, bringing laughter, no stress.
With roots reaching deep and the canopy wide,
Nature's own humor is nothing to hide.

So dance through the greenery, let joy be your guide,
Embrace the whimsy with laughter and pride.
For in this ageless forest, every tree sways,
Breath of delight fills our jubilant days.

www.ingramcontent.com/pod-product-compliance
Lightning Source LLC
Chambersburg PA
CBHW071828160426
43209CB00003B/231